WOMEN OF MYTHOLOGY

GODDESSES, WARRIORS, AND HUNTERS

ATALANTA

Joanne Mattern

Cavendish Square
New York

Published in 2020 by Cavendish Square Publishing, LLC
243 5th Avenue, Suite 136, New York, NY 10016

First Edition

Library of Congress Cataloging-in-Publication Data

Names: Mattern, Joanne, 1963- author.
Title: Atalanta / Joanne Mattern.
Description: New York : Cavendish Square, 2020. | Series: Women of mythology: goddesses, warriors, and hunters
Identifiers: LCCN 2019017590 (print) | LCCN 2019018861 (ebook) | ISBN 9781502651518 (ebook) | ISBN 9781502651501 (library bound) | ISBN 9781502651488 (pbk.) | ISBN 9781502651495 (6 pack)
Subjects: LCSH: Atalanta (Greek mythological character)--Juvenile literature. | Mythology, Greek--Juvenile literature.
Classification: LCC BL820.A835 (ebook) | LCC BL820.A835 M38 2020 (print) | DDC 292.2/13--dc23
LC record available at https://lccn.loc.gov/2019017590

Editor: Kristen Susienka
Copy Editor: Alex Tessman
Associate Art Director: Alan Sliwinski
Designer: Christina Shults
Production Coordinator: Karol Szymczuk
Photo Research: J8 Media

The photographs in this book are used by permission and through the courtesy of:
Cover Painters/Alamy Stock Photo; p. 4 Francois/Perrier/Bridgeman Images; p. 6 Stephen Edwards/iStockphoto.com; p. 7 Henry Justice Ford/Look and Learn/Bridgeman Images; p. 10 Hans Jordaens III/Bonhams, London, UK/Bridgeman Images; p. 11 CW Pix/Shutterstock.com; p. 12 KW.Foto/Alamy Stock Photo; p. 15 Lucian Milasan/Shutterstock.com; p. 16 Matias Del Carmine/Shutterstock.com; p. 17 AlexBF/iStockphoto.com; p. 19 Encyclopaedia Britannica/UIG/Getty Images; p. 20 Archives Charmet/Bridgeman Images; p. 22 Duncan1890/Digital Vision Vectors/Getty Images; p. 24 Denis Kuvaev/Shutterstock.com; p. 25 PictureLux/The Hollywood Archive/Alamy Stock Photo; p. 27 Malchev/Shutterstock.com.

Printed in the United States of America

TABLE OF CONTENTS

Atalanta was one of the strongest and smartest women in Greek myths.

CHAPTER ONE

THE STORY OF ATALANTA

Atalanta was a huntress and fighter in Greek myths. From her birth to her death, Atalanta used luck and smart thinking to help her solve many problems.

Saved By a Bear

Atalanta was the daughter of King Schoeneus. When she was born, the king didn't like that his new child was a girl. He'd

This sculpture of Artemis shows the Greek goddess's beauty.

wanted a son. He took Atalanta to the mountains and left her there.

A goddess named Artemis saw what happened and felt sorry for the baby. She sent a mother bear to find Atalanta and take care of her.

Myth, Fable, or Folktale?

A myth explains why an event like a thunderstorm happens or tells a story about a god or goddess. A fable often has talking animals and usually teaches a lesson. A folktale is a story told for many years by a group of people. It can be about a real person but also have made-up details.

Later, a group of hunters found the young girl. They raised her and taught her many skills. Atalanta grew up to be a fast runner and very good at other sports. She was also very beautiful.

The Boar Hunt

Atalanta went on many adventures. One adventure was a **boar** hunt. Atalanta was one of a group of **warriors** who went to kill a huge boar that was hurting people. Atalanta was the first fighter to hurt

This painting shows Atalanta (*far left*) and her friends hunting the boar.

TELLING THE STORY

No one knows who first wrote down Atalanta's story. Her tale appears in a collection of Greek myths called the *Bibliotheca*. The *Bibliotheca* was written around the second century CE.

the boar. She got to keep the boar's skin and **tusks** as a reward.

An Important Race

As she grew up, many men wanted to marry Atalanta, but she said no. She finally said she would marry the man who could beat her in a race. Atalanta ran faster than every man who tried.

Then, a warrior named Hippomenes fell in love with Atalanta. He asked Aphrodite, the goddess of love, to help him get Atalanta to marry him. Aphrodite gave him three golden apples to use in a race against Atalanta.

At the race, Atalanta ran very fast. She was winning. Then, Hippomenes tossed a golden apple in front of Atalanta. Atalanta ran off to grab it. Every time Atalanta was winning the race, Hippomenes tossed another apple. She always picked up the apple.

This helped Hippomenes win. That meant Atalanta had to marry him. She soon fell in love with him, and the two looked forward to a happy life together.

Atalanta is shown picking up a golden apple while racing Hippomenes.

However, Hippomenes forgot to thank Aphrodite for her help. The goddess got angry and put a spell on Hippomenes and Atalanta. The spell made them upset Zeus, the ruler of the gods. Zeus turned Atalanta and Hippomenes into lions.

ANOTHER STORY: KHUTULUN'S TALE

A story similar to Atalanta's comes from Mongolia. Khutulun was a Mongolian princess and the best wrestler in the land. Khutulun said she would only marry a man who could beat her at wrestling. No one could. Finally, a rich and handsome prince showed up. Khutulun's parents asked her to let him win, but she would not. She won the match and took all of the prince's horses. Later, Khutulun fell in love with a soldier, and they got married without any wrestling matches. She became the leader of the army.

Myths are told in every country.

Books of Greek myths are still popular in schools and libraries today.

CHAPTER TWO

WOMEN IN GREEK MYTHOLOGY

Greek myths are thousands of years old. However, they're still popular today. Students read myths in school. Some books, movies, and video games have characters and stories from Greek myths in them. Atalanta's story isn't studied as much as other myths. However, people who learn about Atalanta like that she was good at sports. She's a role model for people today.

Beyond Gods and Goddesses

Greek myths are full of adventure and exciting characters. However, these tales are more than just stories. They help people understand what life was like in ancient Greece. They show us what people believed and what was important to them, like gods, truth, war, and family.

Greek **culture** is still part of our world. It's interesting to know what these ancient people were like.

Spoken Stories

Storytellers told Greek myths to people. They often weren't written down until much later.

Greek myths also show the difference between right and wrong. For example, the characters in Greek myths do some bad things. The gods punish them for what they do. Readers then knew that those things were wrong to do.

Ancient Greeks worshipped gods in temples like this.

These stories also show men and women who are heroes and do good in the world. They show ordinary people doing difficult and dangerous things. Stories like these helped ancient Greek people be brave in hard times.

Gods often fight monsters in myths. Here, Hercules faces a many-headed monster.

Most of all, Greek myths are fun to read. There's lots of action and drama. Characters accomplish amazing **feats**. Other characters get into a lot of trouble. Ordinary **mortals** and gods and goddesses act the same ways people act today. We can learn from these myths. We can also enjoy them.

Famous Greek Goddesses

There are many women in Greek myths. Many of them are good or helpful. Some play tricks. Some are both good and bad.

Here are a few examples of famous Greek goddesses.

Shown here is a statue of the goddess Aphrodite.

Athena is the goddess of wisdom and war. Her father was the god Zeus. When Athena was born, she was already a grown adult. She wore a suit of armor, like a soldier.

Athena was known for her cleverness in battle. She was a great warrior who fought

Other Ways to Tell Stories

In the ancient world, people learned stories by listening to poets and storytellers, and also through music and plays.

for **justice**. The city of Athens, Greece, is named after her.

Aphrodite is the goddess of love and beauty. Characters in Greek myths like to ask Aphrodite for help in finding true love, like Hippomenes did to win the race and marry Atalanta. Many Greeks worshipped Aphrodite and built **shrines** to her.

Artemis is the goddess of wild animals and hunting. She plays an important part in Atalanta's story. Artemis was seen as a guardian of women. She liked to help them. Like the other Greek goddesses, Artemis showed **qualities** that people still like today: helpfulness, strength, and bravery.

STRONG WOMEN

Greek myths still matter today because the stories still apply to our lives. People have always valued love, beauty, and wisdom. Women in Greek myths have many of these qualities and more. Greek myths also show us that women have power. In history, women have often been shown as weak or helpless. The Greek goddesses and other female characters are strong and powerful. They're just as important as the Greek gods and other men. Myths with strong female characters give readers hope and strength.

Artemis appears with a bow and arrow and animals.

This illustration from 1900 shows Atalanta and the sons of the North Wind.

CHAPTER THREE

ATALANTA TODAY

Today, we still enjoy the story of Atalanta. There are many reasons why we still like it and continue to learn about it today.

Strong and Brave

History often tells us stories where women aren't equal to men. They're shown as weak people who need a man to keep them safe. Stories, poems, and songs often

In one Greek myth, a woman named Andromeda is helpless to escape a sea monster—until a man, Perseus, rescues her.

show women as not smart or not able to make decisions.

Atalanta is the opposite of that idea. She's a strong woman who can take care of herself. She's also very good at sports. She's smart and brave, and she fights too. Atalanta is almost always better than the men. She uses tricks and her intelligence to get out of marrying men she doesn't love. Atalanta is fooled by Hippomenes only because Aphrodite helps him.

How Many Greek Goddesses?

There are more than seventy Greek goddesses in mythology.

A Great Role Model

Atalanta is a role model for today's young people. She shows us that women can be smart and strong. Atalanta isn't afraid to live the life she wants. She enjoys hunting, fighting, and sports, even though they weren't things women usually did back then. Today's girls and boys can look to Atalanta as an example of being true to yourself and being unafraid to take chances.

Atalanta is an excellent role model for young women, like these star runners.

ATALANTA, ARTEMIS, AND KATNISS

Atalanta's story is closely tied to the story of Artemis. Artemis became Atalanta's guardian. She helped her survive. Like Artemis, Atalanta was a skilled hunter who liked being in the wild.

The character Katniss Everdeen is like Artemis and Atalanta.

Today, there are many characters in books or movies that are like Atalanta and Artemis. The best example is Katniss Everdeen. She's the hero of the *Hunger Games* books and movies. Even though the story takes place in the future, Katniss's bravery and skill are exactly like Atalanta's and Artemis's. She isn't a goddess, but she's a strong character young people can also look up to today.

An Exciting Story

Atalanta's myth is also very exciting. People like learning about her childhood. They like hearing the stories of her racing. They also like that she uses smarts to survive. Her childhood was dramatic and full of danger. Her adventures were thrilling. Readers also enjoy the story of the race between Atalanta and Hippomenes.

Atalanta is part of today's **pop culture** too. She shows up in a Japanese comic and

Gods in Stories Today

Artemis and other Greek gods and goddesses are part of the popular *Percy Jackson* books written by Rick Riordan.

Atalanta crouches, tall and strong, in this cartoon illustration.

TV series called *Fate/Apocrypha*. She's also a character in a comic called *Earth-One*.

Even though Atalanta's story is thousands of years old, it still has all the things people enjoy reading about today: adventure, bravery, and love. It's a story that people will continue to share for many years.

GLOSSARY

boar A wild pig.

culture The customs and arts of a community.

feats Tasks that require great skill or strength.

justice Fair treatment under the law.

mortals Human beings who live and die.

pop culture Media or trends popular today.

qualities Abilities or skills.

shrines Holy places.

tusks Long, pointed teeth sticking out from the mouth of an animal.

warriors People who fight in battle; soldiers.

FIND OUT MORE

Book

Korte, Steven. *Wonder Woman and the World of Myth*. North Mankato, MN: Capstone Press, 2017.

Website

Greek Mythology for Kids

penlighten.com/greek-mythology-for-kids

Video

Ancient Greece 101

www.youtube.com/watch?v=6bDrYTXQLu8

INDEX

Page numbers in **boldface** refer to images. Entries in **boldface** are glossary terms.

ABOUT THE AUTHOR

Joanne Mattern has written many books for young readers. She enjoyed reading Greek myths in school and still thinks they are full of adventure today. Mattern has also written about nature, history, sports, world cultures and countries, famous people, and many other topics. She lives in New York State with her husband, four children, and several pets.